Original title:
Fernweh Fantasies

Copyright © 2025 Creative Arts Management OÜ
All rights reserved.

Author: Miriam Kensington
ISBN HARDBACK: 978-1-80567-204-3
ISBN PAPERBACK: 978-1-80567-503-7

Mirrors Reflecting Dreams

In the mirror, a llama speaks,
Wearing socks and clunky old sneaks.
It tells me tales of distant lands,
Where cheese grows tall and laughter stands.

I dive into a swirl of light,
Chasing clouds that glow so bright.
A unicorn waves, daintily prancing,
In a disco ball's radiant dancing.

Shadows of Silken Skies

Shadows float, like silly kites,
Tickling trees on summer nights.
A squirrel juggles acorns with glee,
While singing songs from a rubber tree.

The moon winks at a sleepy cat,
Who dreams of pies and a jazzy rat.
Together they plot a midnight feast,
With pancakes stacked, at least a beast!

Twilight's Gentle Pull

As twilight tugs at the day,
A dancing frog hops on a ray.
It croaks out tunes, all filled with cheer,
While fireflies join, oh so near!

With a blanket made from starry fluff,
We lounge and laugh—not quite enough.
The breeze whispers silly bedtime tales,
Of sock-snatching fish in North Sea gales.

Touching the Winds of Tomorrow

Tomorrow's winds smell like sweet pies,
Riding on feathers and silly sighs.
A parade of penguins, quite absurd,
Marches ahead, not one word heard.

They dance on glimmers of ocean spray,
In top hats and ties, come what may.
With gummy bears playing flute and drum,
We clap along, and that's just dumb!

Whispers in the Wind

In a cafe, there's talk of a place,
Where socks match their shirts, a curious race.
The locals eat spaghetti in shoes,
While singing the news in a jazzy cruise.

A cat with a hat gives a charming speech,
While juggling fish, he's quite hard to reach.
Puns flying high like balloons in the air,
It's a party of giggles, nothing quite rare.

When Dreams Take Flight

I once dreamed I could fly like a kite,
But I just ended up stuck in a fight.
With a seagull named Bob, who stole my fries,
He laughed as he soared, oh, what a surprise!

In my mind, I sailed to a land made of cream,
Where desserts were rulers and sweets ruled the dream.
But all I found there was a melted cake,
That whispered my name, 'For goodness' sake!'

Embracing the Elysian Unknown

In the land where the cows wear cool shades,
And grasshoppers dance in parades,
I stumbled upon a sign that said 'Go!'
But I couldn't tell you if it was a show.

They serve tea with crumpets, but no one's there,
You sip with a ghost—it's quite a rare fare.
He tells me of travels to nowhere and back,
While we both sip our tea from a bright purple sack.

Legends of Lonesome Wanderers

There once was a traveler, alone on the lane,
Who tried to pet clouds and felt quite insane.
He wore flip-flops and socks with great flair,
While debating the merits of fruit in midair.

His tales of adventure are canceled by night,
When he's chased by a raccoon in a bright neon light.
He laughed at his follies and shared them with glee,
While dreaming of places where no one would see.

Melodies of Mysterious Escapes

Under skies where llamas roam,
I danced alone outside my home.
A taco truck, my guide and muse,
With salsa sauce and silly shoes.

In the land of socks and sandals bright,
I twirled beneath a disco light.
An old cat played a lute so fine,
While zebras joined the conga line.

The ocean laughed, it wore a hat,
It tickled every passing rat.
Pirates sang their shanties loud,
As seagulls formed a silly crowd.

Balloons drift high like dreams untold,
Floating tales of fortune bold.
In this land where rules are bent,
I lost my map, but found my scent.

The Call of Inaccessible Dreams

I heard a shout from mountains steep,
A cow in shades of bright magenta leap.
It danced upon a slippery slide,
While hamsters sailed the ocean wide.

In a realm where jellybeans grew,
The rainbows rained their colors too.
A penguin in a tuxedo grinned,
As gummy bears all joined in kin.

A surreal feast on candy chairs,
With giggles echoing through the airs.
The moon wore glasses, night lit bright,
While stars engaged in pillow fight.

In dreams we chase with silly schemes,
Where everyone rides unicorn beams.
So grab your spoon and chase the light,
We giggle on into the night.

Skylines of Forgotten Cities

In cities where the pigeons dance,
With pizza throwers in a trance.
The buildings wear their hats askew,
While squirrels plot their next big coup.

A statue winked with painted eyes,
As children laughed beneath the skies.
The rivers flowed with chocolate milk,
While trees wore coats of fluffy silk.

In alleyways of whirling dreams,
Where laughter bursts like sunlit beams.
The rooftops hid a dance parade,
Beneath the light where jokes are made.

So pack your bags for fun and cheer,
To cities where the skies are clear.
With every step, a giggle springs,
In skylines, we find silly things.

Paintings of Faraway Places

On canvas bright, where colors swirl,
A melon shark begins to twirl.
In forests made of candy canes,
A gopher juggles in the rains.

With brushes dipped in laughter bright,
A hedgehog bakes in morning light.
The clouds are made of fluffy cheese,
While fairies ride the buzzing bees.

In paintings hung on walls of dreams,
Where nothing is quite as it seems.
A windy day brings whispered tales,
Of playful trolls and talking snails.

So let us frame these joyful sights,
In every shade of wild delights.
From faraway lands where spirits soar,
We paint our laughs forever more.

Navigating the Seas of Imagination

On a ship made of jellybeans,
We sail through marshmallow seas.
Chocolate whales jump in delight,
While gumdrop mountains tease.

With a captain made of licorice,
And a crew of silly cats,
We chart a course for pizza pie,
Navigating through laughing hats.

Storms of soda pop arise,
As we dance with fizzy waves.
Navigating through the pastry skies,
Where laughter perfectly saves.

So here we drift in dreamer's bliss,
With the stars as our guide.
Each bite of whimsy, sweet as a kiss,
In this world, let's ride the tide!

Heartbeats of Nomadic Souls

With backpacks stuffed with laughter,
We wander through fields of socks.
Each step a rhythmic giggle,
Scavenging for lost clocks.

From bustling bumblebee markets,
To the corners of cookie lanes,
We chase the sun on roller skates,
Where humor twists like trains.

Our shoes are full of stories,
Of dances in silly hats,
As we map the world's oddities,
Each heartbeat leaving chats.

So let us roam like zany sprites,
In forests of lollipop trees.
With the wind whispering to our flights,
We dash through whims with ease!

The Allure of Untamed Skies

Oh, flying high on feathered dreams,
With cows that moo in rhymes.
They hoot and swoop around the moon,
Playing hopscotch with the climes.

Balloons with giggles in the breeze,
Bouncing like a playful hare.
Chasing clouds that tickle our toes,
While rainbows giggle in the air.

We surf on waves of glitter flies,
As stardust sprinkles around.
In this vibrant carnival of sighs,
Where silly hopes abound.

So let's leap from star to star,
In this carnival of delight.
Our laughter carries near and far,
As we float into the night!

Odyssey of Hidden Wonders

In treasure chests of silly hats,
We uncover quirky charms.
A sneaky raccoon in a tuxedo,
Holds our map in tiny arms.

With a dancing octopus as guide,
We explore the wacky shores.
Where jellyfish play hopscotch,
And giggly seagulls score.

Every step reveals a riddle,
In lands of bubblegum trees.
While mermaids sing tunes of tickles,
We frolic in warm, sandy bees.

So join this quest for laughter pure,
As we wander wild and free.
In an odyssey, sweet and sure,
Where joy is the only key!

Timeless Trails

On a quest for paths unknown,
With a map that's overgrown.
I took a trip to nowhere fast,
But I found a snack that lasts.

My compass spins with glee,
I'm lost but full of tea.
Every turn brings new delight,
Like ducks in a fancy flight.

In the woods, I met a bear,
He offered me a comfy chair.
We chatted 'bout the weather's plight,
Then napped until the stars were bright.

As I wandered all around,
I found my shoes stuck to the ground.
With laughter echoing in the breeze,
My socks were stolen by some bees!

Shores of Solitude

At the beach, I built a moat,
Next to a very grumpy goat.
He wanted sand for his next meal,
But I preferred a tasty wheel.

Waves danced with a silly grin,
While I tried to dive right in.
The splash was more of a big flop,
As my flip-flops went on a swap.

Seagulls cackled in a crowd,
Wishing they were more endowed.
With treasure hunts and silly maps,
They plotted on their sunny naps.

I searched for shells beneath a rock,
But found instead an old sock.
With laughter ringing in my ears,
I made a friend in my weird fears!

Fables of the Journeying Soul

In stories told by candlelight,
I packed a bag for my delight.
With socks and snacks from every place,
I set off for the cosmic race.

I rode a llama, bright and bold,
A tale that never gets old.
With every step, he made a sound,
Like music from the ground, profound.

We ventured forth through valleys wide,
With cheese and crackers at our side.
The hills all whispered sweetly loud,
As if to say, "Join the crowd!"

Upon a cloud, I made a bed,
With marshmallows for my head.
And in my dreams, I laughed and twirled,
Creating chaos in my world!

Reverberations of Dreamt Journeys

I dreamt of trains that fly on high,
With carrots painted in the sky.
We zoomed past llamas in a suit,
Offering snacks of tasty fruit.

My travel buddies wore tall hats,
And danced with very jolly cats.
We juggled pies above the ground,
Creating laughs that knew no bound.

Through jungle vines, we laughed and swung,
With silly songs we all had sung.
Bananas on our heads did rest,
As we proclaimed it all the best!

With echoes of our merry quest,
In every heart, we felt so blessed.
Our feet may ache from journeys long,
But in the end, we find our song!

The Enchantment of Untrodden Ways

In tangled woods where squirrels chat,
I lose my way, wearing a hat.
They point and laugh, 'You're quite the sight!'
I chase my dreams, but drop my light.

A trail of cookies, crumbs of cheer,
Maps in my head disappear.
The path ahead seems rather bold,
But I trip on roots, or so I'm told.

I heard a stream sing a tune so sweet,
Only to find it was my own two feet.
Wandering far to find a place,
But my GPS says 'Lost' with grace.

Through fields of daisies, I prance with glee,
Chasing butterflies who laugh at me.
Adventures loud, but never quite wise,
In the land of daydreams, oh how time flies!

When Stars Become Maps

Under a sky where oddities gleam,
I chart my course by the latest meme.
Constellations dance, misplaced like socks,
Whispering jokes of interstellar clocks.

With a wink and a twist, I take a peek,
At shooting stars that blink and sneak.
They giggle and fall, like plans gone askew,
While I hold a compass that points to the zoo.

Telescopes ready, I point to the sky,
But my neighbor's cat is the culprit, oh my!
I scribble my route with crayons and cheer,
Who knew the cosmos held so much beer?

As I navigate dreams, with snacks in tow,
The Milky Way's just a snack wrap, you know.
To infinity and beyond is the aim,
But I keep returning to the same old game.

Echoes in the Wind

In the gusts that tickle my ear today,
I hear a voice—'Go the other way!'
But strong, I march, determined and grand,
Until I trip over my own two hands.

Whispers drift from trees that sway,
Telling tall tales of a grand ballet.
I spin and dance, but it's truly bizarre,
As I try to tango with a passing car.

The breeze carries laughter, so light and free,
I wave back to clouds who chuckle at me.
Every direction seems filled with jest,
Yet I shrug it off and keep chasing the quest.

Floating away on dreams made of air,
I'm a traveler lost, with mud in my hair.
In a world that spins and swirls and bends,
All I can do is laugh with the winds.

The Allure of Faraway Skies

Oh, the skies stretch far like pizza dough,
Filled with toppings of worries, who'd know?
Up here, I see clouds as fluffy as cream,
With dreams of adventure that bubble and beam.

Mountains and valleys await my bold flight,
With critters down below trying not to bite.
They wave their paws, saying, 'Stay in your lane!'
But I hop on rainbows, ignoring the rain.

Planets swing by, wearing silly expressions,
In tiny spacecrafts, full of fun confessions.
I wave at the stars, all gathered to coo,
Laughing together at things we all do.

Yet as I wander through this vast delight,
I know well enough; I might need to bite.
For the allure of skies, both near and far,
Is tied to a sandwich from the nearest bazaar!

Secrets of Hidden Valleys

In valleys where socks disappear,
And cows have a talent for cheer,
The trees hold secrets, old yet spry,
They giggle as folks wander by.

A squirrel in shades takes a seat,
He's got gossip and snacks for a treat,
With acorns he shares his grand dreams,
Of traveling far to the moonbeams.

The path is a muddle of shoes,
Each step is a dance, no excuses,
With every misstep, laughter ensues,
As we chase our wild silhouettes in hues.

So let's toast to valleys obscure,
With laughter and snacks, we're secure,
Adventure awaits, it's quite clear,
In places where fun's the frontier!

Chasing Silhouettes

I ran with ghosts on a hill,
They whispered secrets with thrill,
"Your shadow is quirky, so bold!"
"It dances like it's never been told!"

We zigzagged through trees with a flair,
Where shadows and sun played a dare,
Mismatched socks were my trophies that day,
In this chase, we laughed all the way.

A cat in a top hat passed by,
With a wink and a twirl, oh my!
He said, "Join the fun, don't be late!"
In this whimsical contest of fate.

So here's to our chase on the run,
Where silhouettes giggle and pun,
In the dance of the shadows we'll thrive,
Sprinkling joy, feeling so alive!

Skylines of Somewhere Else

Above the rooftops where dreams expand,
Lies a skyline that's simply unplanned,
With jellybean skyscrapers all bright,
And clouds that giggle in pure delight.

The sun wears sunglasses, sublime,
As it bounces around like a mime,
The stars play hide and seek at dusk,
In this city of fantasy, fair and brusque.

Birds in bowties hold meetings at noon,
Discussing grand plans with the moon,
While pizza flies in the warm summer breeze,
Bringing laughter like honey from bees.

So let's climb higher, to see it all,
The skyline where imagination sprawls,
In places where giggles create,
Adventures on a whimsical plate!

The Grace of Unseen Places

In unseen places where jests abound,
Ducks wear capes, fly around town,
They quack out jokes, sow laughs with style,
In this hidden realm, we pause for a while.

A rabbit in slippers drops by for tea,
Telling tales of lands wild and free,
Where every flower can play the flute,
And giggles sprout from each leafy root.

We twirl in circles, losing our hats,
Chasing the whispers of giddy chats,
In places unseen, where joy finds its grace,
Every moment a treasure, every smile a trace.

So toast to the laughter that lives out of sight,
In these hidden corners, where spirits take flight,
Adventure awaits in the softest embrace,
In the grace of unseen and wonderful space!

The Map of Lost Places

I found a map beneath my bed,
It whispered tales of places spread.
A haunted castle, a cake so tall,
I'm packing snacks, I might just fall.

With laughter loud, I start to plot,
A dinner date with a talking pot.
Each winding road, a twisty fate,
Just hope my GPS is up-to-date!

A river of chocolate flows for miles,
I'll build a bridge of gummy piles.
In lost places where unicorns sing,
I'll bring my dog—he's quite the thing.

So here I go, with dreams grown bright,
Into the night, on this silly flight.
With every turn, a chance to roam,
In my mind's map, I'll find a home.

Illusions of Wander

In dreams, I chase a flying goat,
She claims to sail on a jellyboat.
Her captain's hat is quite a sight,
We navigate through lemon light.

A parrot squawks my travel plans,
While juggling pineapples in cans.
With every laugh, my bags grow light,
I'll pack my fears; they will take flight.

We stroll through lands of candy rain,
With chocolate rivers, it's insane!
Bears on bicycles ride by fast,
I grin and wave as they zoom past.

At dusk, we bake a pumpkin pie,
What fun it is to reach the sky!
If travel's wild, then bring it near,
With costume parties, I'll persevere.

Footprints in the Sand

I walked along the sandy shore,
My flip-flops squeaked, they begged for more.
I tripped on crabs, they gave me glares,
As seagulls stole my messy cares.

A castle built with crumbs of bread,
I crowned a fish, but it fled instead.
The tide rolled in with salty cheer,
And whispers of snacks were oh so near.

My shadow danced, a wobbly friend,
With footprints drawn that seem to bend.
In every grain, a story swirls,
Of silly pranks from beachy girls.

So here I stand, with bucket high,
I'll build my dreams beneath the sky.
The ocean laughs, it knows my name,
In every wave, a quirky game.

Blossoms of Faraway Fields

In fields of flowers, colors bright,
I stumbled on a bee in flight.
He wore a hat and took a bow,
And said, "Join me—just take a vow!"

We twirled among the daisies tall,
Where laughter echoes, there's room for all.
A picnic spread on buttered grass,
With jellybeans—oh, what a pass!

The butterflies, in pairs, they danced,
To a tune that left me entranced.
I tried to sing, but lost the beat,
And ended up with ants for feet!

These blossoms bloom in far-off dreams,
With silly thoughts and wacky schemes.
I'll wander where the giggles flow,
In every petal, joy will grow.

Reflections of a Restless Heart

A suitcase full of old sunglasses,
Maps from travels never begun,
I wonder if there's a place for my madness,
Where flights are cheap and fun is spun.

The passport's stamped, it's almost due,
Though I can't recall where I last stamped,
I tripped in Paris, ate pasta in Peru,
And got lost in my dreams, just a bit cramped.

I'll dance with a llama, it'll be grand,
Or perhaps a taco that tells me a joke,
On a beach where the sun's like a rubber band,
Bouncing joy to the rhythm of a silly bloke.

Yet here I stand, in an office chair,
While the world spins wildly out there,
My heart's on a train to who knows where,
My desk is my jail, but dreams fill the air.

Chronicles of a Wayward Spirit

Oh, the tales that my socks could tell,
Of trips to nowhere, oh so well,
They've seen too much, now they clash,
Like me and laundry – oh what a thrash!

I googled 'exotic', found a bright beach,
But office work seems too far to reach,
So I pour my coffee and drift away,
To lands where my favorite flip-flops stay.

Ideas flutter like a paper plane,
Dodging paperwork driving me insane,
I wish for adventures, a whimsical spree,
Yet ended up here, with my cup of tea.

So here's to dreams, both silly and grand,
To wandering gently in a soap bubble band,
I'll find you one day, you beautiful place,
Where I can laugh in the sun's warm embrace.

Wanderlust Whispers

My GPS just pointed to a pie shop,
It seems like travel has its funny stop,
Who needs a compass when dessert's in sight?
I'd rather stack pastries than scale a mountain height.

With a map of dreams and a heart full of cake,
I chase after flavors, oh what a mistake!
Yet every wrong turn feels more like a treat,
As I wander the world on a sugar-fueled beat.

I'll sip on some tea while I chase twilight,
With socks that clash, oh what a sight!
My suitcase's bursting, it's nearly outdone,
Filled with the treasures of laughter and fun.

So here's to the air miles that always evade,
And airports where serious dreams often fade,
I'll keep my heart wild and my jokes on rehearsed,
Wanderlust whispers of laughter well-versed.

Dreams Beyond the Horizon

Oh, to sail with the whales on a rubber duck,
Or perhaps ride a snail that's stuck in a rut,
The world's such a canvas of zany delights,
Where daydreaming's cheese keeps the fun in the bites.

I filled out my bucket list on a napkin,
To skydive from clouds while sipping on wax beans,
Yet I'm still here watching reruns in gray,
With popcorn dreams that just float away.

Cactus dancers and disco-fish friends,
Make me giggle as the day slowly bends,
My mind's a balloon ready to burst,
With colors of journeys that I've never traversed.

So let's paint our lives with quirks and with laughs,
As horizons beckon with whimsical paths,
The world is a jest, let's play our part,
In the grand absurdity of a wanderer's heart.

The Call of Distant Shores

A giant crab waved hello,
As I dodged the seagull's swoop.
I tried to dance on the sand,
But tripped over my own group.

The maps I bought, oh so grand,
Showed lands where the sunsets play.
But I ended up in a diner,
Ordering fries in my 'stay'.

Coconut drinks with umbrellas,
And jellyfish made of cheese.
I swam with fish in my dreams,
While wearing flip-flops with ease.

My suitcase burst at the seams,
With souvenirs made of foam.
I write postcards in my head,
But forget to send them home.

Vagabond Dreams

I packed my bags to the brim,
With socks and snacks galore.
In my mind, I tripped on clouds,
Gliding through an open door.

My travel app showed a trip,
To lands both far and wide.
But I wound up in a hammock,
Just napping by the tide.

I chased after a rainbow,
But it led me to a pie.
I devoured slices in bliss,
While clouds floated by and sighed.

I met a goat with sunglasses,
He claimed he's a seasoned guide.
But we just ate all the snacks,
And leisurely strolled outside.

Echoes of Untraveled Paths

In a forest of rubber trees,
I stumbled into a pond.
I thought I saw a dragon,
But it was just a sweet blonde.

Maps were tangled like my thoughts,
Leading nowhere fast, it seems.
I hiked up a beanstalk of dreams,
Falling straight into my schemes.

A squirrel offered directions,
While wearing a tiny hat.
"Just go left at the donut shop,
And follow the sound of fat!"

I found a treasure chest,
Filled with candy and a shoe.
I guess in this odd kingdom,
Adventure's anything but rue.

Starlit Journeys

Late night, I planned my route,
Underneath a twinkling sky.
I sneezed and lost my map,
And sent the stars flying high.

With a backpack full of snacks,
I journeyed on crooked trails.
Found aliens selling space fries,
And worms that told tall tales.

An owl guided my night watch,
Wearing a chubby grin.
"Just avoid the dancing rocks,
Unless you want to join in!"

The stars laughed at my folly,
As I stumbled into trees.
Yet laughter filled the air,
In the land of silly fees.

Vistas of the Heart's Yearning

I dream of peaks with snow so white,
Where llamas dance in pure delight.
The sunbeams tickle my silly hat,
And squirrels sing, 'Hey, look at that!'

I wander through the fields of gold,
Chasing tales that never get old.
A map in hand, I take a leap,
And fall right in a puddle deep.

With each new step, I trip and fall,
My inner compass seems so small.
But laughter fills the air, so sweet,
As I become a traveler on my feet.

I find myself in lands unknown,
Where ice cream cones and giggles are grown.
The world's a circus, wild and free,
And I'm the clown—just wait and see!

Chasing Ghosts of Adventure

Wanderlust takes flight in my head,
A ghost of courage calls, 'Get out of bed!'
But socks go missing, toss them astray,
A haunting chore to start the day.

I grab my map, all creased and torn,
A DIY guide, my future sworn.
Off I go, through thick and thin,
Bloody heck! I've lost my shin!

Past trees that giggle and rocks that roll,
I chase shadows, they take their toll.
But every tumble, every spook,
Turns to comedy in my travel book.

Yet still I dream of lands afar,
With snack-filled bags in a shiny car.
Adventure waits with laughter grand,
Just don't ask me to change my plan!

Veils of Enchanted Landscapes

Behind the mist, the gardens grow,
Where unicorns drink soda flow.
Magic winks with every turn,
And silly dreams, like sunsets burn.

The hills wear hats of cotton candy,
Where jumpy rabbits play all dandy.
I trip through flowers, what a sight!
A fat bumblebee says, 'Hey, you alright?'

With every step, the quirks just rise,
A potion spills, and surprise—pie flies!
I'm caught in laughter, lost in glee,
As daisies wink back at me.

So grab your gear, let's take a ride,
To lands where joy and magic bide.
In enchanted dreams, we'll find our sway,
And giggle till the end of day!

Hues of the Untraveled

In colors bright, the world will spin,
With every hue, I dive right in.
I paint my maps with splashes bold,
And every journey stories told.

Sky blue paths and grassy greens,
Adventures lie in silly scenes.
Orange skies at dusk's embrace,
Turn mundane life to a wild chase.

Each corner turned, a new delight,
Like juggling pies in full moonlight.
I leap through puddles, splash and cheer,
As every mishap draws me near.

So follow me on this colorful spree,
Where laughter reigns, and spirits are free.
In hues of joy, we'll paint the game,
And travel together, ever the same!

The Allure of Untamed Lands

In forests thick, where squirrels plot,
I seek the spot, but lose my thought.
A map I drew with crayon bright,
   I wander 'til I lose the light.

A mountain high, or valley low,
The GPS says I shouldn't go.
With every step, a twist or turn,
To find myself, I must discern.

A river wide, with fish that grin,
I shout, "I'll fish!"—then fall right in.
With dripping shoes and squishy socks,
   I laugh at nature's tangled locks.

Yet through the mess and jumbled ways,
Each misstep brings delightful days.
For in the wild, with all its charms,
   I find myself in nature's arms.

Fantasia of the Unknown

An open road, a car that sputters,
Adventure calls, my heart just flutters.
A sign that says, "Beware of goats!"
I stop to chat, they seem like folks.

An ancient tree with tales to share,
It whispers secrets in the air.
But every time I bend to hear,
A curious bird gives me a sneer.

I cook a meal on random stones,
And hope it won't turn into bones.
With pots and pans, I dance and hum,
But ants decide they want some fun!

Through mishaps, laughter fills the skies,
For every stumble brings surprise.
In lands unknown, I'll roam and prance,
With joy that leaves me in a trance.

Nomadic Reveries

A suitcase full of mismatched socks,
I travel far, with mismatched rocks.
I meet a goat who shares my bread,
And wonder why this path I tread.

A faulty map, my trusty guide,
Leads me right to a muddy slide.
I tumble down, a sight to see,
Where laughing frogs all shout with glee.

A tent that flaps with every breeze,
I swear it whispered 'You'll catch fleas!'
Yet in the chaos, joy ignites,
With starry nights and silly sights.

With each new town, a quirky friend,
And stories that will never end.
In wanderlust, my soul finds glee,
In all the wonders yet to be.

Landscapes of Longing

Upon a hill where dreams collide,
I think of burgers—can't decide.
Should I explore or should I munch?
The local brew is worth a lunch!

The ocean's call, with waves so loud,
But here I sit, just feeling proud.
With sand in shoes and laughing swells,
I build a castle that repels.

A quirky shell, a treasure find,
I wear it proudly, though it's blind.
My pirate face, a sight to see,
With seagulls cawing, mocking me.

As sunsets paint the skies anew,
I dance with shadows, just a few.
Each landscape brings a silly cheer,
With memories that hold me near.

Unveiling Hidden Landscapes

In a land where cows wear hats,
The trees all speak like friendly cats.
I roam the fields in mismatched shoes,
Chasing the whispers of the blue-sky hues.

Under a bridge made of jellybeans,
I hear the laughter of dandy queens.
The rivers flow with fizzy soda,
And squirrels recite the latest moda!

I spy on gnomes with pickled dreams,
Planning parties with jumping themes.
With cupcakes hanging from every branch,
I join their dance and a goofy prance.

Yet in my heart there's a little sigh,
For distant lands where I can fly.
But here I stay, with joyous glee,
In a quirky land, just me and me!

Navigating Nebulous Realms

In candy clouds where rainbows swirl,
I try to catch a giggly pearl.
The moon-walkers tap in fuzzy shoes,
While unicorns share their latest blues.

Navigating skies on swings of light,
Comets chase me in my flight.
But I trip over meringue pies,
And tumble down with silly cries.

With starry maps that shift and sway,
I lose my way, but that's okay!
I dance with shadows, quick and spry,
While fluffy clouds float right on by.

A sprinkle here, a giggle there,
I gather wishes, float without care.
In this silly haze, I simply play,
In nebulous lands where bright dreams stay!

Tides of Longing

The ocean waves are made of foam,
And jellyfish have found a home.
While surfers ride on noodles bright,
Seagulls gossip, take to flight.

I build a castle out of cheese,
And wave to fishes prancing with ease.
But alas! My bucket tips and spills,
I slip on seaweed, do some thrills!

There's picnic blankets made of lace,
Where crabs come out to mingle and chase.
I try to flirt with a lobster bold,
But he just grins and scuttles old.

Yet here I splash, with dreams alive,
In tides where laughter will always thrive.
No distant shores can pull me 'way,
For here in silliness, I'll always stay!

Celestial Cartography

Mapping stars with spaghetti strings,
I catalog what stardust brings.
With wiggly pens that draw so bright,
I sketch a whale that takes its flight.

The Milky Way spills chocolate sauce,
While aliens bounce with a playful cause.
I wave at planets in silly hats,
As they twirl about and dance with cats.

Yet somewhere far, a comet winks,
Teasing my mind with whimsical links.
I chase the light, but trip on air,
And tumble through stars, but do I care?

For in this universe of giggles and glee,
I find a joy that's wild and free.
So let the cosmos swirl and spin,
I'll sketch my dreams and dive right in!

The Draw of Distant Dreams

On a quest for treats galore,
I packed my bags and hit the shore.
I thought I'd find a snack or two,
But ended up in a llama zoo!

With a hat that's way too big,
I danced like an overripe fig.
While llamas laughed and rolled their eyes,
I realized my map was full of lies!

Every fork took me off track,
Found a café run by a quack.
I ordered pie, but what a thrill,
Got served a shoe and a pickle rind spill!

Now I dream of places far and wide,
But trip over my own goofy stride.
In every port, a laugh I'll chase,
With two left feet, I'll lose the race!

Enigmatic Paths

Through winding trails and puzzling signs,
I found a path where sunshine shines.
The locals waved in mismatched shoes,
And sold me hats, not one was my fuse!

A dog named Pickles stole my fries,
While I contemplated pizza pies.
Each trek attracted oddballs galore,
Like a three-legged frog who knocked on my door!

Maps that squiggled made me frown,
As I circled back to the same old town.
But laughter echoed as I went,
Chasing fun, wherever it was sent!

I'll wander onward, quirks in tow,
Collecting stories of places I'll go.
With ridiculous blunders and a goofy grin,
Adventure awaits, let the fun begin!

Lanterns Beyond the Sunset

Under lanterns glowing bright,
I tried to dance with all my might.
Instead, I tripped on my own shoelace,
And did a somersault, oh what a disgrace!

The moon chuckled, wearing a grin,
As I scrambled to get back in.
With shadows twirling all around,
I'm sure I made a very funny sound!

Each lantern on this silly spree,
Wrapped in tales of clumsy me.
I swear a cat laughed as I spun,
In a costume meant for a Halloween run!

Those golden lights of the setting sun,
Brought out giggles and tons of fun.
So here's to stumbles, wiggles, and glee,
Where laughter's the lantern guiding me!

Cadence of Quiet Paths

In quiet woods, I heard a sound,
Was it a bird or a gopher mound?
A squirrel offered acorns with flair,
As I stood, tangled in my own hair.

Each step an echo, a playful tease,
I tried to escape a swarm of bees.
Every hidden nook held a surprise,
Like that bee in my face, oh how it flies!

The tranquil route turned into a race,
As I mingled with worms, oh what a place!
With every stumble, a chuckle grew,
Who knew forests could be so askew?

Yet, with each hiccup, I dared to tread,
The joy of the journey was my only thread.
Through laughter and nature, let's wander free,
In every misstep, find glee for me!

Beyond the Familiar

In a kitchen far away, a cat brews tea,
With a hat on its head, saying, "Join me!"
The toaster's now a time machine,
Adventure awaits, if you know what I mean.

The fridge hums a tune, like an old rock star,
While pickles in jars dream of lands bizarre.
Spices whisper tales from the shelf above,
Each meal's a journey, sprinkled with love.

Battered pots laugh at the way we fry,
As they bubble and dance, oh me, oh my!
A spatula winks like it knows the score,
Flip it! The world's waiting, go, explore!

In this kitchen chaos, laughs do abound,
With every misstep, joy can be found.
The mundane transforms with a twist of a spoon,
In our hearts, those far-off lands bloom soon!

A Tapestry of Travels

A sock slipped away on a trip to Mars,
Left a lonely shoe behind with a few small scars.
It scribbled its tales on the bathroom wall,
While the pants, oh the pants, held an unplanned ball.

Under the bed, a map unfolds,
With lines drawn in crayon and daring bolds.
Join me, it beckons, for a journey grand,
To the crusty old fridge—what a sight to stand!

In the closet, coats whisper secrets untold,
Of windy wonders and nights oh-so-cold.
Scarves do a tango, and hats join the fun,
A fabric fiesta 'neath the bright, glowing sun.

So grab your odd socks, let's venture away,
Past laundry mountains and pillow play.
With laughter as our compass and joy as our guide,
We'll weave our journey with giggles worldwide!

Whirlwinds of Discovery

My suitcase has dreams—it wheezes and sighs,
As I pack it with snacks and some old ties.
Globe-trotting it whispers, with a cheeky stretch,
"Let's leap on a plane! Or just find a sketch."

The cat flops on my passport, claiming its spot,
With a glare that conveys, "Hey, give it a shot!"
I laugh as I trip over shoes in the hall,
At this rate, my next stop is a tumble, not a ball.

Maps are strewn like confetti with glee,
Each alley I wander, so wild and free.
With a donut in hand and a smile on my face,
I'll discover new whirlwinds, in every place!

There's magic in mishaps, I'll fumblingly find,
A parade of surprises—a journey unlined.
The world spins in laughter, pulling me near,
Let's tumble into adventures, without a fear!

Serendipity's Embrace

A coffee that spills brings a smile on my cheek,
As I trip on a pencil, now rolling—how weak!
Yet the laughter that bubbles from sipping too fast,
Turns awkward misfortune to joy unsurpassed.

Lost in the crowd, with a map upside down,
I stroll through the parks, in a frumpy old gown.
I name every pigeon and cheer them along,
Serendipity sings me a silly old song.

With each twist and turn, surprises appear,
A dance with the squirrels, I'll twirl with no fear.
The trees give a chuckle, they know the score,
In this world of wonders, I'm never a bore.

The sun sets in colors I've never seen bright,
As I wander through laughter, into the night.
So here's to the mishaps that come with a grin,
In the embrace of the silly, let the travels begin!

Treasures of Timeworn Roads

On a path where shoes have danced,
I found a sock, it laughed, entranced.
Maps were scribbled with a crayon,
Leading to places where I'd lay on.

Old signs waved from the scruff of trees,
Advertising dreams of endless breeze.
With lemonade from a rusty can,
I planned a trip to see a tan man.

Rusty wheels and squeaky brakes,
I rode a bike that surely flakes.
But I skidded right into a ditch,
With a giggle and a hop, I made a switch.

So here's to roads that twist and turn,
To the silly tales that make me yearn.
Each detour a comic gaffe,
Treasures found in each silly laugh.

Wishes Carried by Clouds

Up in the sky where dreams take flight,
Clouds wear hats, oh what a sight!
I asked a puffy one for a ride,
It said, 'Only if you bring your side!'

Kites fluttered about, holding my hand,
We zoomed through the air, oh wasn't it grand?
A seagull joined with a cheeky squawk,
Together we shared a cloud-walking talk.

Rain drops danced like little flies,
Each splatter followed with comical cries.
I tried to catch them in an old shoe,
But they laughed as I missed, like they always do.

So wishes are clouds, floating away,
Carrying laughter day by day.
With a tip of a hat and wink of an eye,
I chased after dreams, oh me, oh my!

The Lure of Lost Horizons

Chasing the sun on a wooden board,
My legs flailed, I looked like a lord!
Horizons whispered, made me their prey,
'Come over, let's dance, come out and play!'

I stumbled upon an old tin can,
Inside was a map drawn by a man.
He claimed it led to the Land of Snack,
Where marshmallows grow, no need to pack.

With gummy bears as my trusty crew,
We waddled and giggled, feeling brand new.
But the candy trees turned to broccoli,
I'd packed my dreams, just not any folly.

So here's to horizons both lost and found,
Where laughter and whimsy forever abound.
Each adventure brings a silly treat,
Chasing the fun, oh it's such a feat!

Driftwood Diaries

On a beach of spaghetti, I found my old shoe,
The seagulls all laughed, they knew what to do.
With shells as my witnesses, I started to dance,
A waltz with the tide, oh, what a strange chance!

I sailed on driftwood, a brave little knight,
My steed made of flotsam, so gallant, so light.
Crab armies approached, in a battle of crabs,
But I just tickled them, oh how they all flab!

With treasures of seaweed and starfish I found,
I built a grand fortress, my throne made of sound.
The surf was my trumpet, the wind played guitar,
And all of my neighbors were fish from afar!

Now gather 'round dear ones, let's share in my tales,
Of driftwood adventures and unfurling sails.
For every weird moment, there's joy in the mix,
Life's a sassy ocean with plenty of tricks.

Mysterious Portals Await

I found a door hidden in Grandma's old shed,
With polka-dot patterns and a teapot instead.
As I turned the knob, a giraffe handed me tea,
He said, "Have a sip, then we'll dance with the bee!"

Through that strange portal, I bumped into ducks,
Who argued about shoes and their bad fashion luck.
We played hopscotch on puddles of jelly,
While the moon serenaded our wobbly belly.

They showed me their world where socks wore a crown,
And cats played cards, sharing gossip in town.
I tried to fit in, but my dance was a flop,
So I twirled like a pizza, and shouted, "Whoops! Stop!"

But they cheered for my clumsiness, what a big hoot!
In a land where lost things wore mismatched footwear, to boot.
So next time you glimpse something slightly askew,
Remember that laughter can lead you to blue.

Veils of the Vanished

In a land where socks vanished, just like magic tricks,
I found a lost boot, and with it, some crayons.
With scribbles of giggles on the walls of my fate,
I painted a llama, who ordered a plate.

In search of my treasures, I wandered astray,
In gardens of laughter where veggies would play.
The carrots wore hats, the radishes danced,
With laughter abounding, I couldn't help but prance!

But whispers of brussels sprouts chased me around,
"Don't take our dear salad! We're fresh from the ground!"

With a wink and a wink, I tiptoed away,
To find all the things that wished never to stay.

So if you're feeling lost or your socks disappear,
Just chuckle and look for the joy hiding near.
In veils of the vanished, there's always a friend,
With giggles and stories that never will end.

Sojourns in Reverie

I took a vacation to the fridge for a snack,
Where yogurt wore shades, and the pickles were whack.
The butter tried breakdancing, oh what a sight,
And the carrots organized a veggie drum night!

In a dream within dreams, I floated on cheese,
While grapes played the lute, trying hard to appease.
The ketchup was grumpy, but we all held hands,
And danced to the melody of mustard's commands.

I met a potato who claimed he was wise,
He offered deep insights on life and french fries.
With giggles and chuckles, we roasted our fears,
With toppings of laughter, we drowned out our tears.

So take a kitchen wander, chase dreams in the sigh,
For in every odd moment, a joy might just fly.
Embrace every morsel, let whimsy unfold,
In stories of snacks, with laughter yet told.

Wanderlust Whispers

In the fridge, a map is drawn,
A sandwich planned for lands beyond.
Bologna speaks in foreign tongues,
With lettuce sails, my journey's young.

Chasing planes on trees so tall,
Each squirrel whispers, 'Pack your all!'
Carrots wave as I stroll past,
Each bite fuels dreams that'll never last.

Packing snacks and a toy giraffe,
Imagining a comedy half.
With every snack I slowly munch,
I dream of travels past the brunch.

But the couch calls, it's got a plan,
With popcorn lakes, a blanket span.
So here I'll sit, a wanderer bold,
In cozy realms of stories told.

Echoes of Distant Shores

Pizza slices on the shore,
Where seagulls laugh—they want some more.
A beach ball kicks a cloud so high,
'Come surf with us!' they quack, oh my!

Flip-flops fly like thoughts within,
A sinking chair, where dreams begin.
With sunblock battles on my nose,
The ocean waves just want to pose.

Salty snacks, a surfer's fate,
Each wave brings back stories great.
The tide whispers, 'Jump right in!'
But I just munch, and laugh, and grin.

Sandy toes and laughter loud,
Where ducks wear shades beneath a cloud.
My heart's at sea but I just snack,
On gooey dreams with no way back.

Dreams of Untamed Horizons

Cactus Suns and dancing mist,
Adventure calls—oh how I wished.
But first, a coffee—extra strong,
To fuel my dreams where I belong.

With a map made of napkin scraps,
I plot my route through endless laps.
The coffee shop's my launch parade,
With every sip, new plans are made.

Toward mountains made of frosted cream,
And valleys where the gummy bears dream.
I journey forth but must confess,
The nearest snack is my true quest.

So while I wander with a grin,
My backpack holds an endless win.
For every path leads to delight,
When laughter guides the way each night.

The Allure of Untrodden Paths

The garden weeds a tangled maze,
With dandelions dressed in praise.
They whisper, 'Let us roam the streets!'
But first, I need a snack to eat.

A spoon is not a walking stick,
Yet in my dreams, it's magic quick.
Banana peels become my boat,
Sailing through this snack-filled moat.

The fence becomes a mountain high,
Where ants are guides that never lie.
With jelly beans as my supplies,
I scale the heights and touch the skies.

Yet in the end, my real escape,
Is in the couch—a cozy shape.
With laughter ringing in my heart,
Each remote control becomes my art.

The Radiance of Distant Lands

Oh, the joys of jetting out,
With only two socks and a pout!
Chasing views with caffeine in hand,
Dreaming of beaches, oh so grand.

Maps in patterns, like a maze,
I thought I'd find the latest craze.
But ended stuck in a tourist trap,
With sandwiches that gave me a flap!

The spices dance in my nose,
While I sneeze with perfect pose.
The locals laugh, my face turns red,
As I trip on words I never said.

Adventurous hearts, unite and cheer!
For awkward moments, we hold dear.
The world's big laugh is just a flight,
Hop on board, and hold on tight!

Seeking Solace in Faraway Places

In search of peace and quiet space,
I found a cat that's got my face.
It purred like a dream when I gave a treat,
Now we both crave a fancy seat.

Bicycles squeaked while I tried to steer,
Riding like a clown, with no sense of fear.
A wind in my hair, my confidence high,
Until I met mud and that slippery pie!

The locals all point, perhaps they jest,
While I wear my map like a colorful vest.
No solace found in that café chair,
But the laughs echo, I've hardly a care!

Through forests of laughter, I wade in glee,
Dancing with shadows, oh so freely.
With friends in my heart and snacks in my bag,
I bid farewell, with a happy brag!

Journeying Beyond the Horizon

I packed my dreams in a sandwich bag,
Wandering off like a happy stag.
The train's not on time, oh what a plight,
Let's blame it on time zones, just for spite!

The sun, it rises for a great delay,
While I charm the spiders to dance and sway.
Foreign signs feel like ancient runes,
Communication's tough but they have balloons!

Climbing mountains in flip-flop wear,
Falling over, but who really cares?
The clouds they giggle as I take a spill,
But I bounce back up with a hearty thrill!

Each journey brings a funny tale,
Of ricocheting dreams and snacks gone stale.
When sights are missed, it's all in good fun,
For laughter's the prize when the day is done!

The Elegance of Unfamiliar Paths

With a map that's upside down, I trot,
Every path explored, silly thoughts caught.
Stumbling upon elegance in oddest of lanes,
Where the grass tickles and sanity wanes!

Dressed to impress in mismatched shoes,
Pigeons scoff, I've nothing to lose.
The café serves me soup with a wink,
I sip it slow, while I ponder and think!

Oh, the elegance lies in chaos and cheer,
As new hats fly off, let's give a loud cheer!
With each wrong turn comes laughter's direction,
Still searching for style in every reflection.

So here's to paths that make us grin,
To the laughter that rises from all our sin.
When elegance flops like a fish on the sand,
We dance to the rhythm of our own silly band!

Journeys to Unseen Realms

Packing my bags with snacks and dreams,
Off to places where nothing seems.
I'll ride on a cloud, sip rain from the sky,
Chasing twinkling stars, oh my, oh my!

A map made of jelly with roads made of cheer,
I'll wobble on marshmallows, nothing to fear.
Each step I take, a giggle or two,
In lands full of laughter, where wishes come true!

Turtles in top hats play chess with the breeze,
While whispers of wind bring me to my knees.
Oh, what a journey, with each silly twist,
I'll make a big splash in a bubblegum mist!

So here's to the laughs that travel will bring,
With whimsy and wonder, I'll dance and I'll sing.
In realms unseen, let the fun unfold,
With stories of silliness that never grow old.

Starlit Desires of the Soul

At midnight I ride a comet's bright tail,
Cross the galaxy's wind with a tattered old sail.
Laughter erupts from the moons made of cheese,
Where dancing space critters bounce with such ease.

I'll trade my old shoes for rocket-shaped boots,
And converse with the stars about intergalactic hoots.
Their twinkles are winks, a silent applause,
For all of the mischief I'm sure to cause.

Neptune throws parties where raindrops play jazz,
While Saturn's rings spin tales of pizzazz.
With each endless chuckle, I'll gather the light,
And tickle the cosmos till morning is bright.

So take my hand and let's venture afar,
Through nebula jungles, under a moonlit bazaar.
With giggles as currency and joy as our goal,
We'll toast to adventures that feed the whole soul.

Beyond the Familiar

In the cupboard of time, I found a lost key,
To doors that hang slightly askew, you see.
Pants that dance wildly in colors so bright,
Turned out to be hosts of a pajama night!

I stumbled through doorways of spaghetti and fun,
Where meatballs played marbles under the sun.
With giggles and sauce, wear my chef's hat with flair,
Cooking up chaos without a single care!

Hopping on brooms made of sparkles and dust,
I'll race 'round the kitchen with laughter and rust.
Each corner a riddle, each closet a jest,
In this wacky adventure, I'll never get rest!

So let's dive right in and embrace the unknown,
In the land of the silly, I'll make it my own.
With whimsy at heart and mischief in tow,
Life's a funny journey, let's go with the flow!

Embracing the Unknown

There's magic in corners where shadows play peek,
Where the uncommon makes every day unique.
I'll skip down the road paved with gummy bears,
And greet giggling clouds with my wild, silly prayers.

What's that in the distance? A rainbow that's sneezed!
And out pop the colors, all tangled and pleased.
I'll samba with rainbows and twirl in delight,
In this unique universe, everything's right.

The trees wear their hats, while rivers wear shoes,
Every creature I meet has a quirky cartoon fuse.
With echoes of laughter that brighten the sky,
With each step I take, I'll only ask why!

So let's pack our giggles and wander the lands,
With marshmallow maps and our silly demands.
In the whimsical, weird, and delightful unknown,
I'll find my true self in the spaces we've grown.

Threads of Eternal Journey

In a suitcase stuffed, I pack my dreams,
While my socks conspire, or so it seems.
The world outside, a whispering call,
To chase the lizards that climb the wall.

They say, 'Pack light!' I stare, aghast,
As I jingle with knickknacks from my past.
Each trinket holds a story or two,
But who needs stories when I've got you?

A compass spins, oh what a tease,
It points to pizza over Swiss cheese.
With every turn, a puppet show,
Where dreams bend awkward, just like my toe.

Yet here I stand, stuffed like a pig,
Chasing sunsets, or at least a fig.
In a world so vast, with paths unknown,
I'll dance with laughter, forever unthrown.

Ink on Endless Pages

With ink-stained hands, I scribble a map,
Of places I won't find, just a trap.
Each line a joke, each dot a whim,
My dreamland's a comedy, on a whim.

The roads are paved with chocolate bars,
As I plot to reach the candy stars.
But when I arrive, too full to move,
My sweet tooth's the culprit, it's hard to prove.

I pen down thoughts from socks on a spree,
They sneak past my rulebook; who works for free?
Adventure awaits, but first, a snack,
The journey will wait—you best check the pack.

So follow this humor, it's pave with delight,
Craft stories from laughter, day and night.
My ink runs wild, off the pages it leaps,
In a world where the only guide, is giggles and peeps.

Glimmers of the Great Unknown

In the attic of whims, I find my ride,
A bicycle tired from the dreams I hide.
With squeaky wheels, it hums a tune,
As we chase the stars and dodge a raccoon.

Chasing the horizon, a dubious feat,
I pack my hopes and three kinds of meat.
Under a moon that giggles so bright,
I whisper my secrets, out loud at night.

A wink from the cosmos, a sunburned grin,
The journey's a circus where no one can win.
Flip-flops flapping while laughter cascades,
I dance with shadows, as sunlight fades.

In this curious land, nothing makes sense,
But with joy in my heart, I've built my defense.
To seek the unknown, take a chance, say 'hello!'
For laughter's the ticket to places we go.

Hues of Heartfelt Wanderings

In a world of colors, I paint my path,
With brushes of giggles, I unleash my wrath.
Skies blush in pink, the grass wears a smile,
As I meander haplessly, mile after mile.

I tripped over daisies, what a fine sight,
With bees that chuckle and squirrels in flight.
An soggy sandwich from last week's retreat,
Whispers of adventure, or just my defeat?

Every corner turns a new joke to tell,
A slip on a puddle, oh, don't break the spell.
Foliage winks in the sun's bright embrace,
As I skip through the mishaps, a joyous race.

With hues of my laughter painting the globe,
I'm lost in the stories, weaving my robe.
For travel is a canvas, so vividly spun,
With every silly mishap, my heart weighs a ton.

Beneath Infinity's Canvas

The sky stretched wide, a playful blue,
Clouds like sheep, just passing through.
Tangled thoughts of places afar,
But I trip on my shoelace, there goes my car!

Maps spread out like pizza slices,
I chart my course with all the vices.
"Let's go there!" I shout with glee,
But Google Maps just laughs at me.

I dream of mountains, valleys so bright,
While I'm stuck in line for the next flight.
"Properly packed," I claim with cheer,
But my socks are in Spain, and my pants aren't here!

Under the stars, I plot my escape,
To dance with bears or become a grape.
In dreams, I wander, wander, then nap,
Only to wake and find my cat in my lap!

Realm of the Unhindered

In dreams I hop like a cheerful deer,
With a suitcase full of nonsense gear.
Off to the coast, or maybe the moon,
But end up in my backyard with a spoon.

"Let's kayak strong, let's swim with flair!"
But the tide takes my hat far from there.
I start a war with my picnic ants,
While they organize a dance in fancy pants!

With chalk on the pavement, I draw my fate,
A castle, a dragon, and… a plate.
The folks nearby just chuckle and stare,
As I sip my drink and fix my hair.

Globetrotter dreams in this squirrelly state,
"Why not?" I say, while sealing my fate.
In a world where giggles become the light,
Adventure lives in my cat's quirky night!

Whispers of Ancient Trails

The ancient path where travelers tread,
I take each step, then land on my head.
With tales of glories, winding and bold,
My walking stick breaks; it's just old gold!

"Find the hidden treasure," a sign does say,
But all I find is a chipmunk parade.
With whispers of history in the moss,
I trip on a rock, but hey, what a loss!

Rewarded with snacks for dodging the snare,
I feast like a king on a picnic with flair.
"Let's climb that hill!" my buddies all shout,
But I stop for ice cream, and they pout.

Through laughter and giggles, the journey unfolds,
In ancient trails, where laughter molds.
With each wobbly step, life's comedy sails,
As I'm chased by a goat with unyielding gales!

A Symphony of Distant Echoes

A sound of laughter from far-off lands,
Echoes of joy from unwashed hands.
Each note a story, each twirl a tune,
But I step on the cat who's howling at the moon.

Whispers of laughter ride on the breeze,
"Let's dance in France!" I say, with ease.
But I'm tripping over my own two feet,
And my dreams of elegance end in defeat!

A symphony plays in the back of my mind,
Of sunlit beaches and food unconfined.
But I'm stuck on the couch, flipping through shows,
Chasing echoes of laughter that nobody knows!

Yet in silly schemes and flubbed-out plans,
I find my adventure; it surely spans.
With friends and mishaps in this joyous ballet,
Even echoes of folly can brighten the day!

Oceans of Possibility

Sailing on a paper boat,
Chasing dreams with every note.
Seagulls squawk like they know best,
While I'm napping, oh what a jest!

Waves of cheese and shores of fries,
Fish in hats, oh what a surprise!
Tide pulls out my socks and shoes,
Now I swim in silly blues!

The sun's a giant pancake's face,
Not far from my ideal place.
Flip-flops dance, they've lost their friend,
A leggy crab, here 'round the bend!

Ocean's jokes tickle the air,
But all I want are snacks to share!
Mermaids giggle, they're not shy,
As I drift past with a sigh!

The Art of Embracing Dusk

Dusk approaches with a wink,
In my pajamas, I rethink.
Fireflies wear their shiny hats,
While I chase them—who's the cat?

With each sunset, dinner's a game,
Burgers flipping with no shame.
Glow-in-the-dark stars in the sky,
I'm just stargazing, oh me, oh my!

Midnight snacks make me an artist,
Crafting a meal, you can't assist!
A peanut butter smeared delight,
While munching, I discover flight!

So let's embrace the twilight scene,
With giddy giggles, oh so keen.
Bring on the dusk, and the fun it brings,
Where every moment joyfully sings!

Journeying Through Daydreams

On cloud nine, I start to float,
Riding on my sleepy goat.
In a world of candy trees,
I'm picking lollipops like peas!

In my mind, I'm quite the chef,
Whipping up a feast, oh yes!
Pasta twists and rainbow rain,
With each twirl, I can't complain!

Flying fish with silly grins,
Take me where the laughter spins.
A treasure chest of giggles found,
Dance with me on jelly ground!

Oh, daydreams, you sneaky trick!
Your charm catches me so quick.
But when I wake, what do I see?
Just my cat—no magic spree!

Beyond Blue Horizons

Across the waves of tinfoil blue,
We sail on boats made for zoo.
With crayons as our maps to steer,
No jellyfish, just jelly beer!

Beyond horizons, laughter flies,
Pancakes pour from open skies.
Unicorns play hopscotch with me,
While I sip my strawberry tea!

A treasure hunt on a rubber duck,
Why not? We're supercharged with luck!
We find lost socks, and ice cream,
In this wacky, wondrous dream!

So here's to laughs in lands unknown,
Where silly thoughts have really grown.
Let's ride the breeze on cushions bright,
With giggles echoing through the night!

www.ingramcontent.com/pod-product-compliance
Lightning Source LLC
Chambersburg PA
CBHW051629160426
43209CB00004B/567